WILL SOME AFRICAN AMERICANS SIT OUT THE NEXT TWO NATIONAL ELECTIONS?

I think the next two national elections will determine the survival of the USA as a free nation. I also think the next two national elections are the republicans to lose.

The Dems are going to have a big, big problem distancing themselves from their leader which I think they are beginning to do. Everyone knows that the African Americans vote almost always goes ninety percent plus to the Dems. And most African Americans will never vote republican under any circumstance, which I think is a pity.

To me that show a survival dependency mentality that was born in slavery. It blocks free thinking and keeps one from feeling responsible for ones own survival. It leaves us blacks mentally dependent on the good white man (Dems) instead of ourselves for our survival.

Before the "New deal" blacks were more free thinking and independent minded, and even owned far more in wealth and property than today. But, some where after the "New deal" the republicans got branded the enemy and the Dems became our lord and savior. Me, I feel blessed and thankful in spite my troubled soul.

Being mentally dependent minded is why we as a race irresponsible mass kill off each other. We call each other the distasteful "N" word and won't readily support each other in business when there is a choice, in fact we don't really have a survival need to love and care about each other.

That is what this welfare state beast has done to us blacks, it has taken away a survival need for us to need, love, and respect each other. Accordingly to the law of "Natural selection," anything in nature that doesn't have a survival need, it start ceasing to exist until its gone.

Sorry folks, I got carried away, sometimes I start analyzing and go on and on. Now, I was saying the African American voters are the Dems most loyal supporters by far. But, I think the Dems may be skating on thin ice if they think they can kick their leader to the curb and African Americans will still turn out in droves.

Sure, most will never vote republican under any condition, but that don't mean many won't be sitting out the next two elections if not careful, here. That is all, just decided to offer some food for though, and I will leave it at that.

SIRMANS LOG: 12 AUGUST 2014, 1505 HOURS

BEFORE THE "NEW DEAL" THERE WAS NEVER A THREAT TO USA CULTURE, MORALS, AND VALUES!

A lot of people think the USA has always struggled with socialist and others wanting to change or destroy our system of government, and they are right, but there is a big difference in what happening today.

The big difference today is our culture, morals, and values are shot all to hell. With a jury in court or voters in an election no one can truly predict how stupid the outcome may turn out.

before the "New deal" the country went through all kinds of problems and threats but there was never a deadly threat to our culture, morals, and values. Believe it or not, the old saying that no country can afford guns and butter is really true.

That is why Western Europe has already chosen butter, and the USA is now headed that way at warp speed by gutting our military. The destruction of the inner fabric of the USA started when the government seized the social and family provider role for itself during the "New deal."

That was the first dagger stab to our culture, morals, and values. No form of government can survive very long by taking from produces and giving to non produces, in time the load just becomes too great.

The second deadly and fatal dagger stab to our culture, morals, and values was the enacting of the evil 1938 socialist "Minimum wage" law.

That was the coup de grace because a true genuine free floating free market place economy not only safeguards and protects itself; it protects a free nations culture, morals, and values, too.

By enacting an evil 1938 socialist minimum wage law that crippled and took away the economy's power to discipline itself or the nation. That left the USA with a P. . . . of an economy with no power to discipline itself or fight off inflation.

That allowed the government to inflate our currency and grow government like never before. Sure, all of this government financial power boomed the economy and made masses of people happy, but, was it really worth the total destruction of the nations culture, morals, and values. I personally don't think so, but I'm just one lonely neurotic two finger pecking self-made writer.

I will sum this article up by saying the only thing on earth that has a fighting chance of saving the USA from total destruction is repealing the evil 1938 socialist minimum wage law. And even then it will only give us a fighting chance to overcome four generations of liberal clap trap.

Anyone that doesn't think that norms and traditions matter; need to take a look at religions that have mandatory chants or prayers. That is their secret to remaining unchanged over thousands of years. And they won't ever change or deteriorate as long they keep the same norms and traditions going. Yet, we wonder what happen to the good old USA? Duh!

Wise men/women has always known that how you raise your young is not everything, it is the only thing in terms of long time survival, period.
Get a grip America. How can you expect the young to show self-restraint and act responsible when they have never been conditioned to show restraint and act responsible. Duh.
SIRMANS LOG: 06 AUGUST 2014, 1728 HOURS

THE ECONOMY: FIGURES DON'T LIE, BUT, LIARS SHOW CAN FIGURE!
Folks, as an extreme and neurotic self-made writer I don't expect most people to understand my views. To the shallow I may seem negative or maybe even a cold hearted

uncaring hater, but nothing could be farther from the truth.

In fact I believe I am sort of a savior in terms of helping this great nation survive the coming troubled times. My view on all of this great news involving the USA economy: Hog wash, hog wash, and more hog wash.

I heard a guy on the radio say that the USA government is a parasite and when a parasite grows larger than it's host it kills it's host. I totally agree with the above statement, the USA government haven't got there yet, but is awful close. Our welfare state beast is fast destroying our job producing free enterprise economic engine.

Every day the USA government grows larger as our profit driven job producing business host sector dwindles smaller. Never mind what the learned economist and egg heads tell you, I'm telling you it is impossible for the USA economy to overall improve or be saved unless the evil 1938 socialist minimum wage law is repealed entirely.

Man alone can't save a dying economy, the same as a doctor alone can't save a dying patient, but a true free floating free market place economy can and will save itself along with it's host nation if unshackled and set free.

Evil 1938 Socialist Minimum Wage Law Is Destroying USA

Our evil socialist 1938 minimum wage law ties up and restricts our free market place economy to the point where it can't discipline and save itself. And I'm here to tell you I don't care how much tweaking and fine tuning they do nothing can save the USA economy unless it is set free of the evil socialist 1938 socialist minimum wage law entirely.

Good economy news: pure poppy cock, liberals always make things better before an important election, I suspect the cost of fuel will soon be coming down considerably. We all are doomed unless? You know what? We are losing our great USA and it impossible to be saved unless we do what must be done, there is no other way, period.
SIRMANS LOG: 31 JULY 2014, 1821 HOURS

WRITERS VIEW ON THE LAW.
The legislative branch makes the law. The judicial branch interprets and enforces the law according to the constitution. The executive branch carries out the law as is as signed under oath, period.

Now, what the hell should it matter what's one political view is when it come to the laws. The law means exactly what it says in plain

English not some subjective liberal hog wash.

What goes around comes around, and what's up today may be down tomorrow. Freedom can't survive with no respect for the law, period.

SIRMANS LOG: 23 JULY 2014, 0255 HOURS

CONSERVATIVES AND REPUBLICANS FACE A TERRIBLE DILEMMA!

The shallow minded liberals over the years has lied and connived to set the USA on a course to sure doom. In their minds the end justifies the means. And they are too shallow and lack the survival instinct to even know the damage they have done.

Most liberals see no threat or danger in spending and want to increase spending and borrowing to grow government even larger. It is beyond me how anyone can believe you can borrow and spend to no end, but liberals do, I shake my damn head.

They don't see a spending problem with this country at all and if allowed to will spend this great country out of existence, and blame it all on the republicans. My God! What a situation. So you can see, expecting liberals to be responsible and safeguard this nation is a lost cause.

On the other hand, conservatives have an even bigger problem. Conservatives can't seriously plead the case of, "Ignorance is bliss." Conservatives has the capacity and depth to see our great country is on a sure path to disaster.

Conservatives know we are spending ourselves out of existence but face a terrible dilemma on how to stop it. In my view far too many conservatives still want to do the normal right thing of cutting spending and reducing the size of government, wrong. If conservatives do that, they will politically cut their own throats.

Right now that is the worst thing conservatives can do, simply because the liberals has made almost the whole country government dependent to some degree. So, the smartest thing conservatives can do is hold their fire and bide their time before cutting anything.

Talking about controlling spending may work, but to talk about cutting spending and government in this dependent minded climate will definitely keep conservatives out of power.

This writer's position even if no one else agrees with me is conservatives should make it their goal to repeal the evil 1938 socialist minimum wage law. But, never attempt that unless there is a very good chance of success.

Getting rid of the evil 1938 socialist minimum wage law is the only chance of saving the USA from total liberal doom. It shouldn't be planed or talked about just get the power, get in there and do it.

However, there is a big problem, the conservatives disagrees with my views just as much as the liberals.

SIRMANS LOG: 17 JULY 2014, 1605 HOURS

WRITER FREDDIE L SIRMANS SR. DIDN'T WANT TO, BUT JUST HAD TO VENT.

The system can only take so much before it breaks and if that happens we all are in trouble, rich, poor and everyone. I think right now if there is mass disorder our welfare state beast is going for an all out power grab.

The citizen's still has the vote at the present, but, if chaos takes place we may loose that to never regain it. So, when I fill my destiny and keep sending out the stress call to repeal the evil 1938 socialist minimum wage law entirely somebody better listen.

The only thing that can save the USA and individual freedom is a genuine pure free floating free market place economy, period. And the 1938 socialist minimum wage law is the only thing that is blocking that from happening.

The minimum wage law must be repealed or found unconstitutional or we won't survive the coming doom. I promise you I have the supernatural wisdom and survival instinct to know what I'm talking about.

Nothing and I mean nothing is going to save the USA from a total collapse and doom unless the minimum wage law is gotten rid of one way or another. If you don't believe me just keep on living, we'll all soon find out. We all see our system being put to the test; it can only take so much before something snap.

The thing about a true free float free market place is it doesn't choose sides and has never failed to produce an over abundance of whatever is needed. Who you know or who is under the desk doesn't count if you don't produce.

I don't care if you are liberal, conservative, democrat, republican, or whatever, if we don't get this evil 1938 socialist minimum wage law repealed or found unconstitutional we all are going to perish. You disagree, great; we'll soon see who is right.

I know the general public will never understand getting rid of the minimum wage law entirely and I understand that, who wouldn't won't to make and take home more money, I know I do. That is why the very wise founding father made the USA a republic (If we can keep it).

But, what's at stake here is the survival of our country and way of life, and I repeat, there is no way under the sun the USA and individual freedom will survive with the evil 1938 socialist minimum wage law still in place, period.
SIRMANS LOG: 16 JULY 2014, 1639 HOURS

GREAT WRITER BREAKS HIS PEN AND WEEPS!

Folks, I seem to be some kind of freak of nature or the victim of some kind of cruel joke. I am blessed with all of this supernatural wisdom, but no one listens.

I'm jumping up and down, turning flips, screaming and hollering that the evil 1938 socialist minimum wage law must be repealed entirely or found unconstitutional if the USA is to survive.

Its just that simple, our minimum wage law won't allow for a free floating all powerful free market place economy which would discipline itself and the country, too.

Now, our socialist just like in Western Europe is gutting our military to grow bigger government. The U.S. military is the last uncorrupted great institution left in America, and it can't be rebuilt overnight.

In my eyes the future seems so dim. There is no doubt in my great mind, only a true free floating free market place economy can provide the necessary discipline to save the USA. All that is necessary is to get rid of the choking evil 1938 socialist minimum wage law, otherwise there is no hope.

Evil 1938 Socialist Minimum Wage Law Is Destroying USA

To be earnest, deep down in my soul I don't think the minimum wage law will ever be repealed. Too few has the wisdom or the survival instinct to see past their noses now-a-days. I break my pen and weep.

Only the strong survives. The USA is weak in spirit and is the reason we are being invaded. God save the USA.

There is nothing hard or complicated about solving the illegal children invasion problem. The answer is something I have been drum beating on for several years. Maybe there is a divine element about this whole thing.

After all, more people visit a house of worship here in the USA than anywhere in the industrialized world, maybe we are worth saving. The answer to the problem is very simple; just repeal our evil 1938 socialist minimum wage law.

I know, I know, that don't make any sense, where is the connection. You can't see a connection, that is because not everyone has supernatural wisdom and can dissect an economy like this writer can. I'm telling you this type of problem can be unsolvable and may bring the USA to its knees.

You may not agree with the method that I advised, but just remember you have been advised how to solve this problem.

SIRMANS LOG: 12 JULY 2014, 1008 HOURS

FOAMING MAD WRITER RANTS ON, OR, MAYBE HE IS RIGHT?

I, great writer Freddie L. Sirmans Sr. rants on, or, is my super natural wisdom the gospel truth on what will save America. What most people fail to understand is that any way of life will be destroyed in 4-5 generations unless the proper norms and traditions are taught to the young.

During the New deal the government seized the social and family provider role for itself, and from that time since the poor has become totally corrupted. Never in history have the poor murdered unborn babies in the womb, that was always done by the rich and well to do.

The poor has always needed children for labor and to be taken care of in old age. The poor black man was kicked out of the home and that left no one to teach and enforce norms and traditions in the black family unit.

That is why we have all of the insane killing in the black community, that is why there is out of control violence and disorder in the African American community. And it ain't going to get any better until government is out of the social and family provider business, period.

Sure, do gooders will talk, talk it to death, but, will never accept a remedy with any teeth in it.

Since the New deal this whole country is not the same country as before. The mentality is not the same anymore. Gone are the old fashion norms and traditions of depending on ones self. The welfare state has long sent any independent frontier like spirit packing.

Hell, almost half of the country thinks the government owes them a living. It's insane, like the USA government can't ever go broke; where in the hell did stupid thinking like that come from. Not only can the USA and world economy go broke, the USA is already there. The USA is living on borrowed time.

The USA doesn't have a pot to piss in. The USA is almost $18,000,000,000,000,000,000 in debt and counting. Due to our welfare state taking away the need for a strong nuclear and extended family system we have nothing to survive on if we can't borrow anymore, its sheer madness.

There never has and never will be a society or nation that survived without a dependable nuclear family system in place, period. Ours are in ruins. Our moral and spiritual values also are in ruins. Today's norm is murdering unborn babies in the womb on demand. And damn the future, just marry the same sex and ignore the fact that there is no future without procreation, who you love is more important than future survival.

What the hell is my problem, I must be mad or some kind of nut talking all of this normal stuff that was the norm 100 years ago. Your kind is not welcome in the year of our lord two thousand fourteen, go back to the twentieth century.

If the economy crashed tomorrow we have practically no emergency backup bartering capacity to buy time on. Call me a nut, kook or whatever, but, I know I am right on my grave concerns. I beg and I plead, repeal the evil 1938 socialist Minimum wage law now, it is the USA only hope of survival on what's headed our way.

Call me stupid or whatever you like but you ignore my concerns at your own risk. Sometimes, I wonder, Is Washington an imaginary metropolis with a lot of kids behind the wheel.

SIRMANS LOG: 10 JULY 2014, 1732 HOURS

IS THE END NEAR FOR A FREE USA
When the USA is
17,000,000,000,000,000,000 in debt and going a trillion or more deeper each year, you are not going to convince me we have a great

future or even a future at all. The USA is almost totally at the mercy of its lenders.

If nothing else, at least repealing the evil 1938 socialist minimum wage law would give us a genuine true free market place economy and that would assure our survival under all conditions.

Wake up America and get a tight grip on reality because this nation is fixing to have a very, very rude awakening. Liberalism, liberalism, liberalism, I shake my head.

These illegal immigrant people think they are coming to the USA promise land, so, what went wrong, who are to blame. As a writer, I don't know, but, I suspect the hidden hand is the Dems and liberalism.

Love, caring, and having a sense of compassion are good things and is the spice of life. Life would hardly be worth living without these things. However, these predominate feminine emotions make some problems practically unsolvable.

Most of us know what it is like dealing with a wayward family member. Being an enabler almost never helps. When everything else fails most families just let nature take it course. The same applies to the USA as a nation.

Evil 1938 Socialist Minimum Wage Law Is Destroying USA

If the minimum wage law was repealed a true free market place economy would kick in and solve the immigration problem, our jobless problem, our social problems, and on and on.

In the end this immigration thing will boil down to a test of the USA character and survivability, will we pass the test? Not unless the evil 1938 socialist minimum wage law is repealed entirely.

I hope I'm wrong. Almost no one agrees with me on this, still, I stand by my prediction. This whole thing is bigger than Immigration alone, it will determine if the USA survives with individual freedom still intact.

Two primary things have allowed the shallow minded liberals to strike at the heart of our system of government and unless that is corrected there is no way possible for the USA to survive as a free nation.

Number one, by enacting the evil 1938 socialist minimum wage law it gave the USA a p . . . . of an economy with no power to discipline itself. Number two, by government seizing the social and family provider role for itself and not enforcing any rules or conditions, that left no one enforcing discipline and passing on norms and traditions for future generations.

Evil 1938 Socialist Minimum Wage Law Is Destroying USA

A society can't just start over from scratch with each generation and expect to survive very long. The USA is falling apart from lack of sound judgment and character with fewer and fewer people with any common sense.

For example, the law. You don't obey the law because you like it, you obey the law because it is the law. The law is the only thing that protects us all, and especially the poor and powerless. The news media ought to be up in arms with the way the law is flaunted in our faces in high places.

It is impossible for this great nation to remain a free people with no respect for the law like what is happening in the USA today. I rest my case, the jury is still out, we'll see.

No one is above the law doesn't seem to apply anymore in the USA. The bill of rights and individual freedom is something almost unheard of in history before the USA came along, and I use to wonder why.

Now, after seeing what liberalism has done to the USA I understand why freedom is so hard to acquire and hang on to? I just chalk it up as nature knows best. Everything about nature and survival is geared toward struggle.

It is so easy and tempting to just take the course of least resistance and jump on the liberal pie in the sky band wagon. But, I have sense enough to know that no nation can survive without a strong nuclear and extended family system, strong moral and spiritual values, and adequate emergency bartering capacity.

For 6,000 years until the liberal's new deal, governments had the sense to leave the social and family provider role in the hands of the nuclear family unit. Instead during the new deal the USA government removed the need for a strong nuclear and extended family system by seizing that power for itself.

Now, when this whole global economy comes crashing down there is no foundation left to prevent the USA from regressing all the way back to the Stone Age. To me this is common sense thinking, what's wrong with me for wanting to help save my country and survive, shame on me.

Government forcing a evil 1938 socialist minimum wage or price control on a private profit driven business is unconstitutional, period. Of course every worker would be a fool if he/she didn't want to take home more money.

But, force destroys a genuine true free market place economy and results in what's happening in the USA today with no jobs and galloping out of control cost of living. And the really sad part is it's only the tip of the iceberg before total collapse and doom.

SIRMANS LOG: 03 JULY 2014, 1908 HOURS

IMMIGRATION, IMMIGRATION, IMMIGRATION, AND MORE IMMIGRATION TO NO END

Folks, over the years in my writing I have said very little on immigration, in fact I don't think I've ever written an entire article on immigration.

My views on immigration still hold that immigration is a symptom not a cause. And in my view treating symptoms is basically a waste of time and energy. I hear all kinds of conspiracy theories and other stuff on how all of these very young illegal children are flooding into the country and on and on.

But, the way I see it, the cause can be traced directly to liberalism and our welfare state. The survival of our whole system of government was never under threat before 1938 with the enacting of the evil socialist "Minimum wage law," which leads to what I have been Hammering and pounding to no end.

The USA is doomed, the shallow minded

Evil 1938 Socialist Minimum Wage Law Is Destroying USA

liberals has just about succeeded in destroying this great free nation. I love liberals, they are good Americans, it's just that they are too shallow to be trusted with total power.

Many has written me off and dismissed me as that kook or nut that wants to repeal and get rid of the evil 1938 socialist minimum wage law entirely. So be it, I will go to my grave knowing that I'm right on this.

I have supernatural wisdom and can dissect an economy as well as anyone. And I'm telling you the USA cannot be saved unless the socialist minimum wage law is repealed.

My beloved homeland the USA has already started unraveling before our eyes and there is no power on earth that can get us through this as one nation except a true free market place economy. But, it is impossible to have a true free market place economy with a socialist "Minimum wage law" in place.

The minimum wage law must be repealed now, tomorrow may be too late. Once the evil 1938 socialist socialist minimum wage law is repealed the immigration problem will solve itself. With no minimum wage law the over powering suction and attraction that beckons immigrants will no longer exist.

I don't have any proof, but I'm going to go

Evil 1938 Socialist Minimum Wage Law Is Destroying USA

out on a limb and make a bold prediction. I predict soon some nations around the world are going to get rid of any evil socialist minimum wage law entirely and allow a true free market place economy to sink or swim on its own. We'll see.

In my humble opinion there is no such thing as guaranteed lasting wealth anymore; to me it's all a fantasy with no physical connection to reality. Wealth is supposed to represent spent energy and show a direct link to spent energy.

Whoosh, wealth here today but could be gone tomorrow, rich or poor, no one is an exception. If you think this welfare state beast won't seize all bank account to pay it's bills, just keep on living.

Ninety five percent of the population in the USA is living in fantasy land. They have no real concept of private enterprise profit and how it is the life blood of government and our entire survival. I can only express my one man opinion of the sad state of my beloved USA homeland.

I am old enough to remember when the news media and the government placed the law above all else in this great nation. Now, in my view the liberal news media itself is a threat to the survival of our great nation. I believe they are so partisan that the law means very little to them anymore. Why should anyone have total faith in the law anymore when those in high places place politics and outcome above the law?

Again, only strong discipline can save the great USA now. And only repealing the evil 1938 socialist minimum wage law will unshackle our phony P . . . . of a free market place economy, then as a reborn genuine true free market place economy it will start kicking ass and taking names and save this great country from total doom.

All of these people crowding into the USA illegally thinking they are going to have a great future may actually be coming aboard a sinking ship in my view. I'm one that is not one hundred percent for sure that the USA is going to survive as one nation unless some drastic changes are made and soon.

I'm just being honest, Unless the evil 1938 socialist "Minimum wage" law is repealed and gotten rid of entirely I can't see a snowball chance in hell of the USA surviving another five years as one free nation. Hell, I hope and pray that I'm wrong on this.

I understand and can dissect an economy as well as anyone. And I'm telling you the liberal's death grip hold on this country is just too great. And the only power on earth that can break that grip and save the USA is a genuine true free market place economy.

But I repeat, there is a catch, it is impossible to have a true pure free market place economy with a "Minimum wage" law in place. Either the USA repeals the evil socialist 1938 "Minimum wage" law or the USA die. It's just that simple, my intention is not to scare anyone, but that is just the way I see it, sorry. We'll soon see one way or another.

Plus, I got news for conservatives and republicans, cutting spending or government will only get you quickly booted out of office, period. With no warning just do it, just repeal the evil 1938 socialist "Minimum wage" law entirely, and then be still.

A genuine true free market place economy will fight your battle and save this last bastion of true individual freedom left in the world today. It won't be pretty but the USA will survive as one unified free nation.

Otherwise, very soon with no official nation language we might as well kiss a free nation with individual freedom goodbye for another 10,000 years or maybe never to return.

I think the liberals if not provoking something to bring about martial law will gladly seize the least opportunity if it presents itself. The hand writing is on the wall that is why they fear and hate the tea party so much.

Evil 1938 Socialist Minimum Wage Law Is Destroying USA

Boy, the liberals would shut down free speech in a New York minute if they had martial law. With all of the lying and conniving going on in high places the liberal media knows that laws are being broken, but, in their minds it's them against us and to hell with placing the law and country first.

That is why I know the only thing that can save the USA at this late stage is to repeal the 1938 minimum wage law that would bring about a true free market place economy. Only the accountability, responsibility, and discipline that come with a genuine true free market place economy can save the USA from total doom, this I swear.

The other day I seen in the news that the Brooklyn Bridge, Golden Gate Bridge and most of our great bridges and infrastructures were built before the evil 1938 socialist minimum wage law was enacted. Just the facts ma'am, just the facts. So, don't tell me repealing the minimum wage law won't provide jobs, jobs, jobs galore and save this great country.

Look like Benjamin Franklin was right, we had a republic but liberalism won't let us keep it.
SIRMANS LOG; 10 JUNE 2014, 1421 HOURS

THE FINAL SOLUTION!

The struggle to survive: Man and nature has evolved over time and I'm one that believes that if you take the struggle out of survival man will destroy himself.

I think balance in all things assures the best chance of survival. Even love that is not balanced with discipline can be a very dangerous thing, many mothers have cried themselves to sleep at night and even lost a child for that sort of thing. Look at nature itself, with its law of survival of the strongest and the fittest, it shows no mercy, you eat or get eaten.

I believe all human emotions evolved to aid human survival in some way. I think one of the most important things in human survival is the nuclear and extended family system. And the number one reason is it provides the safest and most stable environment to teach the young norms and traditions. Otherwise, each generation will veer off down dangerous and uncharted territory.

Norms and traditions are what maintains order and keeps a society civilized. The "New deal" programs seized the provider role and took it away from the poor traditionally male head of household, but government never instilled norms and traditions in the young like before.

To me that is like a crime against survival. And we wonder why the nation is falling apart. With no norms and traditions being instilled in the young all of the knowledge and experienced passed down from generations was lost when government became a social and family provider.

The USA is now faced with a situation that no amount of knowledge and education can prevent total chaos; only raw nature can save us now. Look at the children invasion situation, it is unsolvable, we are a caring and compassionate nation.

However, Like nature itself according to its laws the weak and faint hearted has the least chance of survival. I apply the same to the USA when the law itself is flaunted and no longer supreme and above all else. In my view we are done as a free people unless the evil socialist 1938 minimum wage law is repealed to restore some sanity and discipline.

In a way it is a blessing in disguised, now, just maybe, the USA will do what must be done if it is to survive. Only one thing can save the USA, "A raw genuine true free market place economy" And all that is necessary to get us there is to repeal the evil 1938 socialist "Minimum wage" law now, tomorrow may be too late.

SIRMANS LOG: 23 JUNE 2014, 2142 HOURS

WHY ARE BOAR HOGS CASTRATED???
The term: "Conception is reality" seem to be more wide spread than anytime in history. On TV they were saying a lady rode to an election victory because of her Ad about her castrating boar hogs.

Wow! As a soon to be 72 year old, that took me all the way back to the late 1940's and early 1950's as a 9 or 10 year old living on a farm in Stockton, Georgia. Today very few young people know how our meats are raised and slaughtered.

Except for the very few our meat comes from the grocery store and that's as far as they ever knows. My family left the farm when I was 14 years old and to this day I don't know the whole story on why they castrate boar hogs before slaughter.

I think it's done to make the meat more tender with a less strong flavor, but, big deal, I'm not about to spend time researching it. Anyway! I would sit and watch as my dad and two or three other men would hold down a big boar hog and castrate him.

I don't know but I'm sure the big factory like farms of today have racks for that sort of thing. But, back then they had to manually hold down the big boar hogs which was no easy task.

Holding the hind legs of a big boar hog can be like holding two powerful jack hammer pistons, and a man can get seriously injury if not careful. Once they would get the boar stable one man would use a sharp knife and make a slit, then squeeze the mountain oyster out and cut the connecting cord, done.

Back then it was before the blow fly was eradicated. I can't remember the name of the medicine they used, all I remember is they mixed it with used motor oil. They had on hand a bucket of this medicine and motor oil mixture and used a stick with a rag wrapped around the end to apply this mixture to the wound.

Back then before the blow fly was eradicated screw worms would quickly get into a wound and do disaster like damage. So, the screw worm medicine was a must and was applied until the wound healed.

City dwellers may not know what the hell is going on here, but, you can bet your bottom dollar that there is a lot of people in this great country that still cherish old norms and traditions, including me. Glory be to God.

Anyone that doesn't think that norms and traditions matter; need to take a look at religions that have mandatory chants or prayers. That is their secret to remaining unchanged for over thousands of years. And they won't ever change or deteriorate as long they keep the same norms and traditions alive. Yet, we wonder what happen to the good old USA? Duh!

Wise men/women has always known that how you raise your young is not everything, it is the only thing in terms of long time survival, period.
Get a grip America. How can you expect the young to show self-restraint and act responsible when they have never been conditioned to show restraint and act responsible. Duh.
SIRMANS LOG: 07 JUNE 2014, 1429 HOURS

DO DUTY, HONOR, AND COUNTRY MEAN WHAT IT USE TO?
When you see all of the ado and outcry of things taking place in the USA today, there is one common thread going through it all, liberalism. And the saddest part of all about the situation is nothing is going to change.

Sure, the "Affordable Care Act" (Obamacare) by law was enacted to be in almost full affect by now, but the Dems have it in "Fool the suckers" mode until after the November election.

The Dems are hoping they can hold on to their majority in the U.S. Senate because if they do we the citizens are going to get all of Obamacare then, and dry too. And all of the terrible misery and hardship ain't going to be pretty. So, if you give someone a stick, why complain when he use it on you, people.

I hear cocky people on the TV all pumped up on believing there is going to be some big republican gain or sweep in November, yet, I'm one not totally convinced. As a self-made writer, I have pounded and pounded to no end that nothing is going to stop this liberal train to doomsday except repealing the "Minimum wage law."

I didn't just crawl out of the wood works to say something stupid. I know without a doubt what the hell I'm talking about; I can dissect an economy as well as anyone. Repealing the minimum wage law will unshackle and set the free market place free to work its magic.

There is nothing else on earth that can save the USA at this late stage; this swamp is just too infested with anti-survival negative liberalism, period. Excess business profit comes only from the private sector and is what provides practically all of the funds for the USA government to survive on.

But, due to taxes, government mandates, and government regulations fewer and fewer businesses are generating profit for government to tax. The cold steel rock hard fact is American businesses don't generate enough excess profit to support our welfare state.

Yet, Washington keeps spending and borrowing by the trillions like the USA has money to burn. Now, you are going to convince me the USA has a bright future, #@%$&*#&, I love you too. Repealing the evil 1938 socialist minimum wage law will in a harmless way slowly bleed off the pressure and stop all of this madness by snuffing out inflation and providing jobs for all.

Sure, it will slowly deflate the economy and no one will earn as much money but everything you buy will drop down to where one can pay their own food and doctor bills out of pocket. But, no one hears my great supernatural wisdom to repeal the minimum wage law, I weep for the only home I know, God save my beloved homeland.
SIRMANS LOG: 05 JUNE 2014, 1429 HOURS

QUICK BASIC ECONOMIC UNDERSTANDING FOR DUMMIES
I, Freddie L sirmans, Sr. as a writer with

great creative thinking ability and almost supernatural wisdom decided to make my suggestion on this VA thing. The VA is socialized medicine which has built in limitations. Still, with strong discipline, responsibility, and accountability the system could be ten times better than it is.

Now, about the economy, I feel I understand and can dissect an economy as well as anyone. So, I'm going to give a brief lecture on how an economy works as I understand it. In my view consumer inflation is something bad and dangerous, sort of like riding a tiger; the problem is staying alive when getting off.

Maybe that is why modern day economist doesn't want inflation to end. No matter what one may think an economy is made up of only two players, a seller and a buyer. Sure, it may look modern and complicated but over all an economy is very simple.

Long before a currency was invented the early economies were based on people trading and bartering with each other. But, you can't trade or barter unless you have what someone else wants. If you had a lot of potatoes and no one wanted any then you were stuck. So, as you can see some type of a currency was needed to trade for whatever one wanted.

However, with a currency also came profit,

which was a God send to the growth of government. Government was now able to take directly it's cut of profit in the form of taxes or take possessions and auction them off for the profit.

Profit is generated when a seller sells a product or service for a fee more than the cost in labor to produce the product or service. And the difference between the two is called profit. When a seller continues to sell products and services for a profit he is now a proprietor and operating what is called a business.

A business is only a medium of exchange to generate a profit, if a business fails to generate a profit it cannot exist and must close. Government itself is not part of the economy but what it does greatly influences the economy.

In a society or nation government is a must to provide internal and external protection and to do the things the people can't do for themselves. But, one thing government should never do is become a social and family provider. That is like a nation feeding on itself.

Once government becomes a social and family provider it is only a matter of time before its demand for more and more taxes become endless. Government becomes like a junkie on the streets for a tax fix until it destroys the very source of its own survival, which is the profit generated by businesses. Are we there yet? Nope, but we are getting awful close.

To finance government being a social and family provider that money must come from a private business directly, or from the wages and possessions of it's employees. But remember, a business doesn't pay taxes, people pay taxes. A business is just a medium of exchange to generate a profit.

The working people and those who pay taxes is who pays for our welfare state. And the load has become too heavy, only our massive debt load is keeping us fed. And who knows when the bottom will drop out of that and doom us all.

In the early days of business a big problem was finding the capital to grow and expand. That problem was solved when someone came up with the idea of dividing a business into shares and selling the shares as stock. And then along comes compound interest and economics took on a life of its own.

Sure, all of this other stuff changes things, but in my view it still boils down to just two players, a seller and a buyer.

Again, I repeat, there is nothing on earth that

can save the USA as a dying nation except a genuine true free market place economy. But, it is impossible to have a true free market place economy with a "Minimum wage law" in place.

For the shallow minded the "Minimum wage law" is all about wages and a paycheck or how much one is getting paid. If the minimum wage law was repealed tomorrow I doubt there would be much sudden change in what people get paid.

There is no "Maximum wage law" on what an employer can pay for labor. To get better workers you got to pay better wages. It still holds true, you get what you pay for. My focus on the "Evil 1938 socialist Minimum wage law" is the mechanics of what it does to the discipline of a free market place economy at work.

Any forced wage or price control no matter how small kills the discipline in a free market place economy. All of the great production power and abundance of everything in a free market place economy is all due to its discipline. You get paid what you are worth to the business, not what the government says you are worth.

When the evil minimum wage law was enacted in 1938 it took the discipline out of the USA economy and our whole society has been slowly falling apart ever since. And only repealing the minimum wage law will give the USA a fighting chance of surviving the destruction of our nuclear and extended family system, our moral and spiritual values, and lack of any emergency backup bartering capacity.

What is called a free market place economy here in the USA today is actually a phony p.... of a true free market place economy. The USA economy of today lacks any true discipline to purge out gross inefficiency and moral decay. Discipline is what gives purpose to life.

There is no lasting success, enjoyment, or anything in life without discipline. I beg and I plead to you, bring back the discipline the USA economy once had. Repeal the evil 1938 discipline snatching law that forced this socialist "Minimum wage law" on needy vulnerable victims.

"Forcing" anything in a free market economy is socialist no matter what good is intended because force destroys the inherited power and discipline in a free market economy.

A "Minimum wage law" is purely a disguised socialist tool parading as something good, and surely, it fools all but the very wise. The truth of the matter is if it's so good, why force it on the people; make the "Minimum wage law" voluntarily.

Now, to shift gears, Global warming and Climate change are just liberal Hoaxes to try and take attention away from their nation destroying policies. Besides, the USA acting alone couldn't make a difference even it did matter.

The fact is "Matter" cannot be created or destroyed anyway, meaning the earth is design to constant change and adapt. Spending even one second on climate change in my view is a waste of time.
SIRMANS LOG: 30 MAY 2014, 2014 HOURS

SOME WANT A BALANCE BUDGET AMENDMENT AND CONSTITUTIONAL CONVENTION
A constitutional convention in today's climate is a dangerous and bad idea in my view. A balanced budget amendment is unneeded and a waste of time in my opinion. To me the system itself ain't broke, it's just been hijacked by the liberals.

The role of being a provider in itself calls for wielding power over others. The federal government shouldn't be a social and family provider in the first place, that is our problem in a nutshell right there. Let me say up front, I think a balance budget amendment or anything else is a waste of time for anyone thinking it is going to stop reckless spending.

As long as government is a social and family provider nothing is going to stop reckless spending until government is voted or kicked out of that role. Sure, there are many that believe a balanced budget amendment will solve the problem, but they don't truly understand human nature.

The force and drive for reckless spending is the nature of the beast, and it comes with the social and family provider territory. It is like honey to a bear, at least conservatives won't go wild, but with liberals there is no restraint when it comes to spending someone else's money.

You see, we all too some degree has become dependent to this beast, our welfare state. And as long as this beast is in the role of super social and family provider we as dependents are going to allow our leaders to beg, borrow, and even steal to keep it fed. Look at what this beast has already done to our values and morals, and we haven't seen nothing yet.

The truth is we the citizens are like little dependent children trying to demand a drunkard irresponsible parent stop reckless spending on booze, it ain't gonna happen. We the citizen gave up our independence with the "New deal" when we allowed this beast to seize the social and family provider role for itself.

Before the "New deal" seized it, for over 6,000 years the social and family provider role has always belonged to the nuclear and extended family head of household, who dutifully instilled self-restraint, respect for authority, and respect for norms and traditions in the very young.

This must be done to safeguard the future and future generations, but, when the federal government seized the provider role for itself it failed to carry out these duties. That is why our norms, morals, and values has gone to hell, and we are going to loose this great country unless the minimum wage law is repealed entirely. That will give the free market place back it's power to save this great nation, nothing else can do it.

The basic personality of an individual is shaped by the age of ten. That includes self-restraint, a respect for authority, morals, values, and society norms. So, if no one is instilling proper norms in the very young, how in the hell can anyone expect the USA to stay civilized and crime free.

There is a survival reason why norms and traditions are so important. It is like everything in life, there is no substitute for experience. Having norms and traditions safeguard us from doing a lot of dangerous and stupid stuff that leads to disaster.

The young has always thought they knew all of the answers and older folks were behind the times and didn't know what was going on. Not realizing that their parents had passed that stage years ago and certain things never change.

The young is 100 percent of our future. Liberal policy starting with government seizing the social and family provider role and making our economy impotent by adding a minimum wage law is destroying the USA from within. I beg and plead, please repeal the evil 1938 socialist minimum wage law now, tomorrow may be too late.

The states did something even more stupid than the people giving up their independence, the states gave up their power to control this welfare state beast. Before the seventeenth amendment the two state senators in Washington were appointed and worked for and reported to their Governor and state legislature. They served their states self-interest, not all of these extreme environmental and other liberal groups.

The federal government's role is to collect taxes, protect the nation internally and externally, and do only the few things the people can't do for themselves, period. When the federal government becomes a social and family provider it starts feeding on itself and cannot possible survive over four or five generations in that role.

People I'm telling you our time is up with having a provider government, everything is already up-side-down. So, I'm telling you until the federal government is either voted out or kicked out of its social and family provider role no constitutional convention or balance budget amendment is going to stop reckless spending.

In our current climate it seems obvious that the federal government will never be voted out of its social and family provider role. That means the only way the USA is going to be saved from total doom is for government to be kicked out of the provider role. I'm crazy enough to believe that will soon be done.

In a free nation there is no force greater than a true genuine free market place economy, not even the law. A true free market place economy has the power to break this doomsday grip the welfare state has on this nation and give the power back to the people. But, let me add, it is impossible to have a true genuine free market place economy with any amount of a minimum wage in place.

A minimum wage law de-nuts or castrates a

true free market place economy and makes it practically useless discipline-wise. And what the USA have now is not a true free market place economy, but a phony powerless effeminate punk of an economy that is about to self-destruct.

Only repealing the evil 1938 socialist minimum wage law will take the shackles off and allow a genuine true free market place economy to rise up out of the ashes like phoenix and save our dying nation. So, here is the priority of what it is going to take to save the USA from total doom.

Repeal the minimum wage law entirely, its just that simple, repeal and the USA survives, continue on as is and it will soon be over.
SIRMANS LOG: 21 MAY 2014, 1626 HOURS

POLITICAL POLLING OUGHT TO BE OUTLAWED OR AT LEAST BANNED 3 MONTHS BEFORE MAJOR ELECTIONS.
I shouldn't even be writing this article because I have already wore out the subject of talking about the evi 1938 socialist minimum wage law. "You can't get blood out of a turnip." Yet, demanding that businesses that are barely surviving raise wages is trying to do just that.

It says a lot, we as a nation has just about

lost the knowledge of what it means to be a free people. Liberal policy has almost destroyed our sense of self-determination to somehow make it on our own ability.

I will say it again louder; our USA swamp is just too big and too crowded in liberal thinking, liberal beliefs, and shallow liberal judgment. And this nation can't possibly survive very much longer unless this swamp is drained by repealing the minimum wage law.

Ninety five percent of the American population has fell prey to this cock and bull lie that our super sugar daddy welfare state provider will always be there to take care of us from cradle to grave. No one thought like that before the "New deal seized the provider role from the nuclear family head of household.

Two liberal policies must be undone before this great country can be saved from total liberal destruction. And we are way pass the stage of no return, first the minimum wage law must be repealed or else the USA economy will soon fall into total chaos.

Sure, I totally agree with these good decent people that a person ought to be able to earn a livable wage. But, most of these people have never run a business and doesn't have a clue as to why they shouldn't be paid more.

However, I excuse these people, but I don't excuse America's leaders and the news media.

True, the liberals did hijack the country with the "New deal." Still, the duty in a republic form of government is for leaders to educate the public and bring them along on what is in the best interest of the country.

It is not to circumvent the founding father's intent by insane political polling to pander to an uninformed general public. Political polling ought to be outlawed or at the very least banned three months before every major election, period.

There was a time in the USA when a woman could walk through a poor or middle class neighborhood at midnight with a purse and no one would harm her.

Yes, that was before 1938 when "New deal" liberal policy seized the social and family provider role from our nuclear and extended family system. And the final coup de grace was the enacting of the "Evil 1938 socialist Minimum wage law."

It is taking around eighty years for the final death rattle. But, it is similar to a poisonous snake biting a rat, the snake doesn't get in a hurry chase, it knows the rat won't get too far. It is the same with our evil 1938 socialist minimum wage law; the USA economy cannot and will not survive very much longer, unless the minimum wage law is repealed, period.

PS: The fact is repealing the "Evil 1938 socialist Minimum wage law" will enable the American people to make a livable wage, but it is so sad that I am one of the very few with the wisdom and depth to see it. God, I ask in your name, save my beloved homeland.
SIRMANS LOG: 16 MAY 2014, 0049 HOURS

I BELIEVE IT'S TIME FOR MEDICAL SUPERVISED FLOGGING TO BE TRIED
I believe societal-wise four or five hard lick on the rear will do more to reduce crime than ten years in modern day prison. That would be especially true with the young and first time offenders. And the big advantage is its practically free with no housing and caretaking cost to the tax payers.

Flogging is nothing new and it works. There is a lack of real discipline in the early raising in most homes today. That lack of discipline is a failure to instill self-restraint which makes one aware of consequences. I think it is time the whole USA criminal justice system considers experimenting with flogging seriously.

The prisons nationwide are already filled to

the brim. Daily as I listen to the local news there is smash and grab, break-ins, muggings, and crime, crime galore. Hell, I know I'm barking up the wrong tree, because oh no, we are too civilized to stoop to something so primitive as flogging.

I'm just saying we are being over run by crime and taking care of all these law breakers are just too expensive. I'm not talking about the sadistic cold hearted murders and rapist; of course they must be kept locked away. Folks, I'm a writer and I call a spade a spade and tell it as I see it.

It is not going to get any better folks, either we control crime or it's going to control us.
SIRMANS LOG: 08 MAY 2014, 2239 HOURS

WRITERS OPINION ON PUTTING ETHANOL IN GASOLINE!
I think putting ethanol in gasoline was one of the cruelest hoaxes ever pulled on the American people. Anyone that have an older or any car that is seldom driven is going to have problems.

With ethanol in it gasoline deteriorates so rapid that the gas tank needs draining after a few months or so if not used. Plus, sooner or later it is going to drive the cost of all corn products out of sight.

I have an old classic car that I seldom drive and I gotta find me some ethanol free gasoline somewhere. Sometime later, shame on you Freddie Sirmans Sr, for thinking there is still individual freedom left in the USA to buy ethanol free gasoline!

Hell, how was I to know that it is mandated by the Feds that ethanol free gasoline can no longer be found in this great free country. I guess I will just have to drain all of the gas out of my old classic car and keep the tank empty or run the hell out of it. Wake up America!

They do have perservatives one can add to the fuel, but it is still a dumb idea putting a vegetable product in gasoline.
SIRMANS LOG: 12 MAY 2010, 0029 HOURS.

STIMULUS, STIMULUS, DUMB, DUMB, I THINK!
To me a stimulus package is like putting paper money down a rat hole. All it does is make a bad situation worse. When a nation is spending almost twice as much as it is taking in it is insane to think more spending is the answer, it is impossible to spend your way out of debt.

I truly understand how an economy works

and to me the answer is very simple. The first truth is government spending is the problem and until that is recognized and admitted there is no saving the USA and global economy. What congress and the president needs to do first right now is recognize that this nations survival is at stake and act accordingly.

Instead of going on silly financial wild goose chases, void all regulations on businesses right now. Next, completely eliminate the minimum wage. Next, set up temporary emergency government run commissaries, government run housing in all these empty buildings, government run clinics, and use tokens or script for all who qualify for these government services.

Next, stop all government spending except for military and essential government only functions. I know to most this line of thinking will be seen as insane, but, I assure you the stimulus path will lead to guaranteed doom for the USA, or we end up as a debt slave owned and controlled by foreigners.

My way to salvation is only a suggested path to take it doesn't have be word for word like I say but the path is a way out of no way, a word to the wise should be sufficient. God bless America.

PS: This path will set the USA economy free and guarantee without a shadow of doubt that entrepreneurs and the free market will save this
great nation with freedom intact, nothing else can do that.

We must place all of our faith and trust in the proven ideology of the "Free market place at work.
SIRMANS LOG: 1 SEPTEMBER 2011, 0846 HOURS

ECONOMICALLY IGNORANT SUCKERS, I'M TRYING TO EDUCATE YOU!
The minimum wage debate is a main reason why the founding fathers made the USA a republic form of government. Ninety five percent of the American people are in favor of raising the minimum wage.

I believe there should never have been a forced evil 1938 socialist minimum wage law in the first place. And the only way to save the USA from total destruction is to repeal the minimum wage law we have now entirely. The ninety five percent supporters see the minimum wage only in terms of making more money at work, and a few see it in terms of costing jobs.

However, as a deep great thinker, in my view that hardly touches the surface as to the effect of a minimum wage law. The "Minimum wage law" of 1938 was one of the last "New deal" programs put in place.

Next to the government seizing the family provider role for itself I think forcing a minimum wage law on a free market place economy is the most dumb and destructive thing there is. Sure, the effect is not instantly but it is a poison pill like cancer that slowly eats away the inner fabric of a nation until there is nothing is left.

Look at the USA today we are practically just a shell. Our culture has been ripped to threads, our morals and spiritual values are up-side-down, and we have almost no emergency fall back bartering capacity in case our currency collapses. And the really sad, sad part is ninety five percent of the population thinks I'm stupid or some kind of nut case.

That's a judgment call, and having a minimum wage law in the first place have damaged our judgment like almost everything else. A true free market place economy has never failed to produce an over abundance of jobs, food, or what ever is needed.

But, the powers that be has never liked a true free market place economy simply because if you don't produce you don't survive no matter who you know or b... And the real secret to the success of a free market place even though few realize it is its discipline.

Authoritarian type governments keep moral and culture rot from getting out of control by brute force, but, in a free nation the only way to keep moral decay and culture rot from getting out of control is through a highly disciplined true free market place. Free countries think they are too civilized to flog law breakers or give other harsh death sentences.

I will end by saying: Enacting a evil socialist minimum wage law takes the discipline out of a free market place economy, thereby giving a free country a death sentence. We are now reaping the harvest planted from the "New deal" seeds. I rest my case.
SIRMANS LOG: 02 MAY 2014, 1540 HOURS

THIS MINIMUM WAGE THING MAKE IT LOOK LIKE THE MAYANS MAY NOT BE TOO FAR OFF THE MARK AFTER ALL
The reason why 95 percent of the USA population can't understand the destruction of our minimum wage law is due to a lack of perspective. The thing about economics is you can never understand it looking at it piece meal.

It must be viewed in the whole which includes culture, morals, spiritual, trade, and the use of a currency. Who wouldn't like to make more money, I certainly would (I heard that!). But, in economic terms just by the stroke of a pen forcing any wage control or a raise in wage control on a free market place economy means its total destruction.

No, its not instant death, but the die has been cask and about four generations into the future sun set will be almost impossible to avoid. Now, our time is up. we have had our four generations and our inner fabric have been ripped to threads.

The cancer has for all practically purpose destroyed our culture, our morals, our spiritual values, and any emergency bartering capacity to survive on. In fact we are left with just a shell with all of our inner fabric eaten away or destroyed.

And, the really, really sad part is 95 percent of the USA population has become too dependent minded and shallow to realize it. Lord have mercy. And even worse the last and only thing that could give the USA a fighting chance of survival is totally ignored, sad, sad, sad.

Abolishing the evil 1938 socialist minimum wage law entirely is our last and only chance of surviving as a free nation; yet, economically ignorant people are going to raise the minimum wage control lever even higher which will speed up even the little time we have left.

I'm at my wits end, more and more it looks like the Mayans may not have been too far off the mark after all. Mans actions always determines his future. However, it's never too late to do the wise thing.
SIRMANS LOG: 25 APRIL 2014, 1249 HOURS

LATE ENTRY:
There is a reason why I chose repealing and getting rid of the minimum wage law entirely as top priority to save the USA from total doom. You see, the USA is now a swamp totally infested with all kinds of negative anti-survival swamp things.

It's just too much in here, so, the best and wisest thing is to just drain the entire USA swamp. Out of hundreds of negative anti-survival forces that can take down this great nation I'm going to name three or four.

These forces are a threat to long term survival because we may no longer be able to produce a big enough future generation to carry on.

Example: We already have mass use of birth

control pills, mass use of abortions on demand, and thanks to the courts we now have mass use of men marring men and women marring women. What else is new?

Now, you are going to convince me that there is no long term threat to this great nation, #@&%*#$@, I love you too. That was only a sample of what growing more powerful everyday in this swamp.

Repealing the minimum wage law in one sweep nationwide will in a harmless controlled manner drain this swamp. This will kill two birds with one stone, by starving the welfare beast out of power and setting the free market place free at last to save us all.

And as a bonus the provider power will revert back to the nuclear family and the people where it has always been until the "New deal" seized it.
SIRMANS LOG: 26 APRIL 2014, 1940 HOURS

CONSERVATIVES VERSUS OBAMACARE
Never mind trying to fix Obamacare or anything else concerning it. My advice to conservatives is get the hell away from the ball. The liberals are behind late in the fourth with little time remaining and punting out of their own inzone.

To conservatives never mind a fair catch or running it back, just get the hell away from the ball. And don't try anything fancy just go ahead and run out the clock with things that has been proven to work for conservatives.

To hell with the pollsters or how boring it becomes, just stay with lower taxes, more jobs, and strong national defense. And for God sake stay away from details until after the election no matter how much the liberal press pisses and moans.

Otherwise, the liberal press as always will paint conservatives as mean and uncaring, which always highly influences our gullible electorate. That only worked in the past because of pseudo conservative tactics and being all over the map.

Stay with your proven strong running game, it wins championships.
SIRMANS LOG: 22 APRIL 2014, 1344 HOURS

PS: My advice, stay away from Obamacare. In my view it stinks, it smells, and is just one big gutter insurance mess. And you know what they say about the gutter, if you crawl down in the gutter for a fight, no one comes out smelling like a rose. Stay the hell away from it; let it rot away on its own.

Conservatives must anchor down with lower

taxes and more jobs without details instead of going all over the map on side issues. That's because for the next two years the liberals are going to keep some kind of racial or extreme side issue going to turnout their main base.

Conservatives can't lose if they pound over and over like mad men/women, more jobs and lower taxes. That will build base trust instead of selling ones soul for a vote they'll never get. Even many liberals will vote for someone they trust and believe will actually fight tooth and nails for more jobs and lower taxes.

The real problem with the Republican Party is they don't trust the American people and the people don't trust them in return. Why should the people trust the Republicans because in the last presidential election they ran from the words "Lower taxes" like it was the plague? When Republicans no longer fight for lower taxes they don't deserve to win in my view.

Like it or not, pollsters or not, if the Republicans ever expect to win the big one again, the people must believe without a doubt that they will fight tooth and nails for more jobs and lower taxes. The people already know without a doubt that the Dems are going to fight tooth and nails for bigger government and higher taxes.

If you want to throw caution to the wind and live in the moment, then go ahead and join the Dems, as for me, I will go down trying to do what I can to help save my country from insane spending.

SIRMANS LOG: 23 APRIL 2014, 1640 HOURS

SICK AND TIRED OF BEING SICK AND TIRED
I get so sick and tired of sheer economic ignorant people thinking raising the minimum wage is going to help this economy. In fact the only thing that is going to save this economy from total doom is out right repealing and getting rid of the evil 1938 socialist minimum wage or any wage control entirely.

Since 1938 the minimum wage law has allowed the liberals to get control of the USA economy which is a little over four generations. Like I have said many times you can get almost any cock-eyed economic system to work for four or five generations, then its sun set time.

Sure, the intention was to do good, but, economic-wise installing a minimum wage or any kind of wage or price control on a free market place economy is dumb, stupid, and destructive, period. It is a dagger right into

Evil 1938 Socialist Minimum Wage Law Is Destroying USA

the heart of a free market place economy and it ignites inflation, then after four generation it is impossible to keep inflation from spinning out of control.

I'm going to say it even if the egg heads and Keynesian economist never will. Raising the minimum wage just may be the straw that breaks the camels back and sends what's left of the wobbly-kneed USA economy over the cliff.

I'm just sick and tired of people who should know better keeping the people economically ignorant just to go along to get along. We need leaders calling a spade a spade. And I'm telling you the only way to improve the lives of the people and save the USA economy is to set the free market place free, not cripple and weigh it down even more with a higher wage control.

I'm just tired of the economic ignorance of it all to see my beloved homeland go down the tube with liberal policy. And to this day they are still lying and fooling the people with pie in the sky for all. Don't get it twisted, I love liberals, they bring happiness and make the world a far better place, who else will make sure Bambi is always safe and protected.

It's just that liberals should never have total power because most lack depth and live in the moment in my view. However, there is

Evil 1938 Socialist Minimum Wage Law Is Destroying USA

nothing innate about being a liberal, many has been converted to a conservative over night when a mugger slammer one upside the head or burglarized one's home.

Being a liberal is mostly a lack of survival awareness more than anything else. Discipline is what makes one more aware of what's a threat to survival and it instills in one what is call a survival instinct. And one with a strong survival instinct automatically knows and feels what is a threat to survival including the unborn, too.

That is why those with strong survival instinct just knows and feels without being told that certain things are a threat to survival. However, since the government kicked the poor black man out of the home and failed to instill discipline itself most young black males lack self-restraint and has very weak survival instincts. This government act has all but totally destroyed the black community and is fast engulfing the entire nation.

In no way am I putting down most young black males, in fact under the circumstance most are overcoming great odd and turning out well and successful. And in the big liberal controlled inner cities that's totally gang infested the odd are stacked overwhelmingly against most young black males, yet many still escape to Morehouse and other great institutions.

Many black women complain about black men in general, and my answer is always the same as a question. Who do you think shaped and molded the values of most black men today? You know the answer to that.

Excuse me folks, I just got carried away; I just had to vent; now I feel better. Still, the minimum wage law must be repealed and gotten rid of entirely, now, tomorrow may be too late.
SIRMANS LOG: 19 APRIL 2014, 1211HOURS

TO SEE OR NOT TO SEE, HALLELUJAH!
Who are you going to believe, me or your lying eyes? A wise man knows there are times when you should cut your losses and move on. The USA is the only home I know and I feel duty bound to do what I can for the survival of my homeland.

I know the repeal of the evil 1938 socialist minimum wage law is the only thing that can save my country. You can lead a horse to water, but you can't make him drink. It's the same when I plead and I plead, please repeal and get rid of the minimum wage law entirely.

I'm at my wits end; you can't make a man see something right before his eyes until he wakes up. There has been countless cases where people have suffered bad accidents or other dreadful things, yet, said they were glad it happened.

They said things right before their eyes they could never see before they can now see very clearly. You can call me a nut, kook, or whatever you like, but I can see clearly things right before our eyes most people will never be able to see.

That is because I have paid a severe mental price through a life long mental battle and struggle. Yet, I have no monopoly on pain, struggle, or suffering, I'm just thankful to have my life health and strength, Hallelujah.
SIRMANS LOG: 17 APRIL 2014, 2103 HOURS

THE USA VOTERS STILL HAS THE POWER TO DE-CLAW OUR WELFARE STATE BEAST
Okay, ignorance is ignorance no matter how you look at it. And that is what has happen to the USA since the government seized the social and family provider role from the nuclear family unit. There is a world of difference between learned intelligence and wisdom.

To set up a system of government like we had before the "New deal," it took men of great wisdom. In fact, almost everyone of that era had good wisdom and strong survival instincts due only to just the struggle of day to day living.

Today most independent minded people in the USA know we are in trouble and can't survive with the way our welfare state beast is out of control. But, they don't have a clue as to the real answer, they just want their freedom and rights back.

The American people still have the voting power to reset this country back on course but don't have the wisdom or survival instinct to see what is right in front of their eyes. I'll lay it out, there are two main things that happen around four generations ago that brought this country to the condition it's in today.

Sure, during the great depression the very poor and handicapped needed government help. But, government should never have become a social and family provider handing out free money on an individual basis.

(1.) Once that mistake was made the system destruction die was cast. And until that deadly mistake is corrected and the nuclear family unit is restored to power the USA cannot and will not survive. That was the birth of our welfare state which has practically destroyed our economy, our culture, and our moral and spiritual values.

Men are marring men and women are marring women, all while mass murder is taking place within the womb. And 90 percent of the USA population accepts this as normal, what am I missing here, is it too late for the USA.

(2.) In 1938 the last of the "New deal" programs was put in place, the evil socialist "Minimum wage law." That act was a dagger in the heart of a true free market place economy; it awakened the sleeping monster called inflation. Otherwise, a true free floating free market place with no controls is like a liquid, it will always find its own level.

But, not any more, inflation and the U.S. economy is now like a car with no reverse or a hot water heater with no pop off valve, that is what the minimum wage law has done to this once great USA economy. So, I will advise anyone thinking about saving the USA, until these two boogie men is caged and sent packing that is an impossible task.

You can go to a flat tax or enact any law; our welfare state beast will laugh at you, smile, and then go spend another trillion in debt. But, repealing the minimum wage law to this beast is like the iron cross or the silver bullet riding in on a white horse as destiny to save the greatest nation to ever exist.

SIRMANS LOG: 15 APRIL 2014, 1449 HOURS

WHO TRUMPS, A TRUSTFUL AND RESPONSIBLE CONSERVATIVE OR A BIG GOVERNMENT LIBERAL?

The hand writing is on the wall that liberals are on their way out of power. To conservatives, never count your chicks before they hatch. There is a reason why liberals has taken over and dominates news, education, and nearly every institution in America.

These extremely intelligent super aggressive shallow minded people will not let anything stop them from getting and keeping power. If conservatives think these people are going to lose power without pulling out all of the stops they may be in for a rude awakening. No matter how advantageous the Obamacare nightmare may look it is still not a done deal to defeat the Dems.

Here is why, approaching half of the voting population has a dependent mentality like a child to his mother in favor of the Dems. In that group are the African Americans we know is going to vote 95 percent in favor of the Dems. And the females to a lesser degree we know are going vote a big majority in favor of the dems.

Plus, the predominately liberal news media

we know is going to focus on and praise every extreme liberal side issue. And on the other hand we know the mass media is going to demonize almost everything the conservative's tries to advance. There, you see for yourself where the advantages lie.

Myself, I am an independent, but with conservative leaning. I think listening to the pollsters is the reason the republicans has lost the last three presidential elections. Things like faith and trust may not show up in polls. No one beats the liberals at their own game.

Everyone knows the Dems are going to hand out goodies and tax and spend to kingdom come. And everyone knows that republicans once were for lower taxes, more jobs, and strong national defense. But, not any more, no one knows what the republicans stand for now, except trying to out pander the Dems...

I'm sure that is the main reason the republicans lost the last three presidential elections. So, my advice to the Republicans: Obamacare alone can't be depended on to defeat the Dems, because everything including the kitchen sink is going to be thrown at republicans.

Forget about trying to out pander the Dems, besides, no one will believe and trust you anyway. Just lock on like a pit bull to only three or four proven winners such as, lower taxes, more jobs, and strong nation defense.

When elections can't be won with these three things, it won't really matter because that means freedom is lost forever in America. Just stay with three or four proven winners, otherwise being all over the map allows the liberal media to rip you to threads.

I believe there is still a majority of independent minded American voters that will choose someone they truly believe will lower taxes, provide jobs, and keep our country strong over a big government candy-man.

All the republicans need to do is stand for lower taxes, more jobs, and strong nation defense. And stay the hell away from details because that is a fools game the liberals will try to trap you in to no end.

But, in order for the republicans to be trusted as a political party ever again it must be trusted without a doubt to stand firmly for at least one or two things come hell or high waters.

Everybody knows without a doubt that the Dems stands for goodies and freebies, and taxing and spending. So, forget about trying to out give the Dems because they will gladly give away the store and the country too to stay in power. You are not going to out give

um or out spend um, ever.
SIRMANS LOG: 12 APRIL 2014, 2240 HOURS

IT IS IMPOSSIBLE TO SAVE USA ECONOMY AS LONG AS GOVERNMENT IS A SOCIAL AND FAMILY PROVIDER, PERIOD.
People that don't understand economics or how the free market place actually work automatically think getting rid of the minimum wage is dumb and stupid and will increase our hardship, wrong.

In fact it is just the opposite in reality. Sure, given time one won't make as much money, but, it will bring earnings and the cost of living back in balance. And $5.00 will buy a weeks worth of grocery.

I must have said it a thousand times. Unless the government is voted out or kicked out of its social and family provider role somehow there is just no way the USA can survive very much longer.

I hear people on the air talking all the time about every way one can imaging on what will save America. Again, I repeat a thousand and one times, it is impossible to save the USA as long as government is a social and family provider.

Government as a social and family provider is like incest, it is a system that feeds on itself. Sure, almost any economic system can last four or five generations then its lights out. What happens then is it can't get around a law of nature.

Sooner or later everything that exists must go through a life or death, or boom or bust cycle. The evil 1938 socialist minimum wage law won't let the economy carry out a natural boom and bust cycle. Therefore the negative anti-survival forces have grown too powerful in the USA.

Now the USA is in a position where moral decay and culture rot is going to take us out if a collapsing economy doesn't get to us first. The way I see it to save the USA it will take a two step process.

The main focus is the government must abandon or be voter out of its social and family provider role or all is lost. But, that ain't gonna happen. So, by repealing the minimum wage law that should kill two birds with one stone, kick the government out of the family provider role and save the country too.

The power must be restored back to the people. It belongs back to the strong nuclear and extended family unit where it has always been for over 6,000 years until the "New

Deal" came along. Repealing the minimum wage law will bring about a controlled orderly rebirth that will save our nation.

Otherwise, its no longer a matter of our welfare state collapsing, it is a matter of how many months, or even day we have left. I know I stand almost alone on knowing only repealing the minimum wage law can save us.

I beg and I plead to my fellow man/woman to demand we repeal the minimum wage law. If you disagree with me on repealing this law, God bless you, almost everyone else does, too. Still, someway some how it will be repealed, it must.
SIRMANS LOG: 03 APRIL 2014, 1934 HOURS

THEM MEAN OLD EVIL REPUBLICANS AND CONSERVATIVES!
Almost everyone is in an uproar about the USA government giving up control of the Internet. However, I believe hardcore liberal lions and lionesses want the U.S. to give up control of the Internet. And they want it bad.

I think they view talk radio and conservative Internet as a big threat to their domination and that will be a first step on silencing these blabber mouths. They don't know how yet, but I believe they believe that will be a foot in the door.

So, in my view these people will do almost anything if it will stop them mean old evil Republicans and conservatives from telling on them.

SIRMANS LOG: 31 MARCH 2014, 2258 HOURS

GREAT THINKER FREDDIE L SIRMANS SR. GIVES HIS VIEWS ON THE SURVIVAL OF THE USA ECONOMY

Folks, I decided to do a little brain storming on the state of USA survival. We are in it now, but, I will say it again this idea of a global economy is a fool's game in my opinion. It will never work unless one country had total domination, and that ain't gonna happen.

These globalists have come up with the North American Free Trade Agreement (NAFTA) and a host of other job sellouts in my view. Now it is water over the dam, saving the country is top priority now. I blame liberals for the dire condition the USA is in today, but, what good is that going to do, none.

Overall the "New deal" programs were intended to do good and help the people have a better life. However, human nature is what it is. Power corrupts and absolute power corrupts absolutely. No one political party alone has brought the USA to the dire situation it is in today.

It is not about right or wrong or getting righteous people in place, it is about getting people elected that have the common sense to do what have been proven to work. In other words it is the system in place that really matters. And that is the unforgivable sin I blame on the "New deal" programs they destroyed the system the founding fathers left in place.

Now, we have a corrupted and run-a-way system that allows lying, twisting of the law, and all kinds of anti-survival things to strive. Here are the two main things that brought about our run-a-way economy. Number one, the new deal programs seized the family provider role for itself and failed to carry out the discipline and responsibility of being a provider.

That act caused our culture to deteriorate with each succeeding generation, now in the home if it feels good do it. Plus, once government becomes a family provider, economically it starts feeding on itself and eating its seed corn. It takes around four generations to totally self destruct but by then the culture and all the inner fabric of the country is gone and there is nothing to rebuild on.

Evil 1938 Socialist Minimum Wage Law Is Destroying USA

Right now, every thing else aside, the only way I see the USA having any chance of surviving is to repeal the minimum wage law, and that will only give us a fighting chance. The number two thing is what gives fuel to our run-a-way economy.

In 1938 the "New deal" programs enacted the evil socialist "Minimum wage law" that removed all free market place dampers and allowed government to then tax and spend to no end. In other words with a minimum wage law in place there is no way to balance the cost of living to earnings. End result is fewer and fewer working to take care of more and more not working.

That process destroys the culture, the nuclear family, small farmers, and home gardeners, and then when it all collapses we have no foundation to rebuild upon. I will now touch on today's political situation. Due to Obamacare it looks like the Republicans may take total control of congress in November 2014.

If the liberals hadn't destroyed our true free market place system I believe the USA could have out lasted the Roman Empire but I'm afraid unless a miracle happens we are done. The Roman Empire lasted a thousand years. The Republicans think they can cut spending and save our out of control run-a-way economy, wrong.

I will say it again; the USA and Western Europe welfare states cannot be saved. Cutting spending piece meal here and there will only make the economy worse. It will also piss off half or more of the people. That will only guarantee the shallow minded liberals will be voted right back in control. Yet, cutting spending is the course the Republicans are locked on.

For the most part liberals mean well and want to care for everyone, it's just that human being are not just cogs in some big machine. Humans being are motivated by reward and punishment and responds accordingly. But, most liberals are too shallow to understand that, still, I love them and they are good Americans.

If the government was kicked out of it social and family provider role that would solve our run-a-way out of control spending problem, but that ain't gonna happen. So, here are the cold steel rock hard facts, if the USA is ever going to be saved only conservative have the will and sense to do it.

I think the anti-survival opposition has grown so powerful that the conservatives have time for just one shot at our survival target. And if the target is missed the anti-survival death grip will never be broken and that means sunset for the USA. The target I'm referring to is repealing the minimum wage law.

Conservatives need to tread water and hold off on any major spending cuts until after 2016. Then after 2016 repeal the minimum wage law once and for all. Repealing the minimum wage law won't be any peace meal deal, it will deal with the entire USA economy nation wide in one sweep.

That will allow the poor and middle class to pay out of pocket for their own food and medical bills. And it will mean jobs, jobs galore for all nationwide. Sure, one won't make as much money but the lower cost of living won't require one to need as much money.

However, I believe this but the problem is very few conservatives agree with me on anything. Like it or not there is no other way for the USA to survive.

As for the very, very poor and needy the government will need to establish government run commissaries, housing, and clinics for them. And use tokens or scrip for all who qualify.

God, I ask in your name save my homeland, the USA.
SIRMANS LOG: 29 MARCH 2014, 1852 HOURS

CONCERNING TRAIN OPERATORS AND OTHER WORKERS ON MUST STAY AWAKE JOBS:

There is a no cost very low tech technique to prevent one from falling asleep. It cannot not be used in every situation, but will certainly work where there is a hard flat floor. I have personally used this technique many times on a must stay awake job.

Many years ago when I worked as a Federal Firefighter sometimes in the middle of the night we would have to standby on welding's or other situations. Just sitting there most of the time no problem, but a few times I did use this low tech technique to make sure I stay awake.

This is how the technique works, just hold in your hand car keys or any small object and if you start to doze it will drop to the floor with a loud enough sound to snap you back alert. First rule, immediately pick the item back up.

Here is a little brain storming to inventors: Come up with something to hold in one hand that will emit a signal every time it is dropped.

SIRMANS LOG: 26 MARCH 2014, 2011 HOURS

NOTE OF FACT:
As I have said before, being $17,000,000,000,000,000,000 in debt means the USA will soon be sold off piece meal to foreigners. Otherwise, eventually the USA will be taken over without even a shot being fired unless the evil 1938 socialist minimum wage law is repealed.

This giving away control of the internet is proof enough of my dire predictions. I believe if you scratch deep enough our national debt has compromised the USA in some way. The minimum wage law has all but destroyed our culture and it must be repealed before nothing is left.

Culture wise the USA is fast approaching the point of no return where there is not enough people left with the judgment or common sense to remain a free people. I plead for my mother land, repeal the minimum wage law before it is too late.

SIRMANS LOG: 15 MARCH 2014, 2101 HOURS

ONLY A TRUE FREE MARKET PLACE ECONOMY CAN SAVE THE USA.
There is no substitute for experience no matter what it is in life. There is an old saying that youth is wasted on the young.
Experience is one of the most valued things in life, yet, economy-wise it is totally ignored.

Another old saying: When everything else fails, read the directions. Look at our economic problems, we are in no mans land, uncharted territory, or some other metaphor, yet we ignore what has been proven to always work, a true free market place.

The reason we ignore over 5,000 years of proven experience on a system that has never fails is because we as human beings are controlled by logic and self-interest. That is why I know without a doubt that it is impossible to save the USA economy unless the minimum wage law is repealed.

The USA can go to a flat tax or any other kind of tax system, or enact any law, but nothing is going to stop government from taxing and spending the USA out of existence except repealing the minimum wage law. It's simple, once government seized the provider role for itself there is no peaceful way out without facing the pitchforks.

Besides, once the government tasted the god like power of being a super provider, they got drunk on it and will never voluntarily give up an inch of that power.

SIRMANS LOG: 14 MARCH 2014, 2249 HOURS

WHY THE MINIMUM WAGE MUST BE REPEALED IF INDIVIDUAL FREEDOM IS TO SURVIVE!

Very few people have the wisdom to see it, but the reason I drumbeat so hard on repealing the evil 1938 socialist minimum wage law is: It will kick big government out of its seized social and family provider role and return that role back to the nuclear family where it has been for over 5,000 years.

Rebuilding the strong nuclear and extended family system is the only thing that is going to prevent the USA and western civilization from collapsing back to the Stone Age. The whole welfare state foundation revolves around the minimum wage law being in place, otherwise, a true free market place economy wouldn't allow all of this inflating and printing of worthless money.

The reason why a true free market place economy with unrestricted competition never fails is because of its strong discipline. And the key ingredients for that discipline are letting the market place determine free floating labor and price levels. So, when government set any price or labor level in a free market economy it distorts the process and sends discipline out the window.

When the "New deal" programs seized the social and family provider role from the nuclear family provider that was bad enough, but the slow death pill for individual freedom was the enacting of the 1938 minimum wage law. Now, there is nothing that can stop our big government beast from taxing and spending this nation out of existence except the repealing of the minimum wage law.

Even that may not save us but it is the only thing that will give us a fighting chance to survive, because all of our survival tools such as a strong nuclear and extended family system, strong moral and spiritual values, and adequate small farmers and home gardeners for bartering capacity when money is worthless are almost nonexistence.

Anyone with an ounce of economic understanding knows the USA economy is going to totally collapse or the country will be sold off piece meal to foreigners, the powers that be will never tell you that, but I just did.

I'm fixing to say something that if I had any sense I would never utter a word on the subject, but so be it. Here goes, I and a lot of people wonder where my great supernatural wisdom comes from. I never went past high school and have never read any books on economics or very little on anything else.

Now, to destroy any credibility I have left if I ever had any in the first place. This is where I suspect my great wisdom comes from: Brace yourself, I believe in reincarnation and suspect I was a German or Austrian scientist in a past life. So, how do you like me now?

PS: Remember, I write what I believe, and believe what I write. However, occasionally I may throw in something solely for shock value. In this case, you decide, if I'm for-real.

SIRMANS LOG: 08 MARCH 2014, 1015 HOURS

I'M CURSED WITH THIS GREAT WISDOM, AND WONDER, WHY, WHY ME OH LORD, AND AGAIN, WHY NOT ME!

I know beyond a shadow of doubt that government as a social and family provider has all but totally destroyed the USA, yet I am so alone on realizing that fact. We have been fortunate to survive this long with government playing that role, but the price to the nation has taken an awesome toll.

It has all but totally destroyed our culture, our moral and spiritual values, and any adequate emergency bartering capacity with small farmers and home gardeners in case the economy collapses. We have almost no small farmer and home gardeners like what got this nation through the Great depression.

We have no means of surviving except back to the Stone Age. Government as a social and family provider for all practical purpose has all but totally sucked the life blood out of this once great independent nation. I write, I preach, and I plead to deaf ears over and over on what will save this great nation, all to no avail.

But why, oh Lord why, why won't someone listen when I plead that repealing the evil 1938 socialist minimum wage law will save this great nation by freeing the people to save themselves and the government, too. What good is a raise in the minimum wage when it's just more money for government to take, waste, and squander away. Plus, it will definitely driver up the cost of everything we buy even higher.

After the minimum wage is raised and you sum it up the cost of living will be ratcheted up another notch, which will be a net loss to the poor and middle class, duh. Sure, back before we had a minimum wage law people made far less money, but, $5.00 would buy nearly twenty times what it will today.

If you was lucky enough to make it to middle class you could afford a saving account and didn't have to live from pay check to pay check. Again, we must repeal the minimum wage law or we die. It is sheer ignorance not to realize the minimum wage law must be repeal. The roads, bridges, sewage system, and infrastructure all over the country is falling apart and only repealing the minimum wage law can we get it done, duh.

The liberals seized the social and family provider role from the traditional nuclear family head of household in the "New deal" era. It is impossible for government to survive very long as a provider to the people because every penny the government gets is taken from the earnings of the people in the first place.

Governments sole role in a free society is to take only enough tax money from the people to provide internal and external (military) security for the nation. And to take care of the interior and do only the things the people can't do for themselves, period. Government as a provider is like eating your seed corn and drinking your priming water, sheer ignorance.

Just the day to day survival in days of old taught most people this simple basic wisdom. Back then nature and the elements were relentless and unforgiving. If you failed to teach your young responsibility and accountability you may not have any left.

This great wisdom I have is a curse to me because I see so clearly what must be done, yet, my beloved mother land marches on and on to sure doom. I plead and I beg do what must be done to survive, repeal the minimum

wage law before it is too late.
SIRMANS LOG: 04 MARCH 2014, 1554 HOURS

DUMB, DUMB, AND DUMBER!
Folks, I'm a self-made writer and sometimes I wonder why I keep writing. I do comment on something's I have no business butting in on. But, thank God I can still comment without disappearing in the middle of the night, at least for the time being.

A proposed alternative heath care plan by the republicans: Stupid, stupid, stupid, here we go again. Just like I think Romney had his election won, all he had to do was lock down on two or three things. Things that republicans never lose on, but no, he just like McCain and Dole tried to out pander the liberals and Dem's.

All he had to do was stay on "Lower taxes, more jobs, and strong national defense," instead of being all over the place pandering and appealing to those that will never vote for a republican in a million years. If he had stayed with the said three things he would have gotten the three million republican votes that stayed at home.

Now, I hear about some supposedly conservative plan to present an alternative health care plan to Obamacare. Dumb, dumb,

dumb, how dumb can one get. That would be a toss up to a gleeful socialist press and they would hit it out of the park.

They would focus on it like a laser and drumbeat on how bad it is. All you would hear from them is this is what you can expect from them mean old republicans. What is going to win the 2014 election is future expectations and right now anything is better than more Obamacare.

So, the dumbest thing conservative can do is present a target, good or bad. Never forget, the mass media is socialist and not free and objective anymore. All they need is a real target then one way or another they will make it bad. And that will be the only future expectation as far as the media is concerned. My advice to conservatives, if you have a plan shut the hell up about it until you have the power to install it, in this hostile climate.

"CURSE OF THE "NEW DEAL"
Starting with the "New deal" the liberals seize control of this great country and it's been down hill for them ever since. How they did it, they took the tax payers money and bought vote by handing out goodies, and is still doing it.

It allowed them to gain and keep power, sure, the republicans slip in occasionally but liberals control this great country. Look at our food supply, there are too few people raising and growing food in the USA. That comes from having a evil 1938 socialist minimum wage law.

That is wage control and any wage control won't let wages seek its own level in our free market place economy. Having a minimum wage law guarantees that the USA economy can't be saved no matter what is done. You can enact any law, make any tax change, still, nothing can save the USA economy as long as we have a minimum wage law in place.

The reason is a free market must have some means of balancing itself and a minimum wage law prevents that. The reason the prices of everything you buy is so high is because government subsides prices by giving out tax payer's money on an individual basis.

That-a-work until the whole thing spiral out of control which won't be very long, now. A minimum wage law is like closing off the pop off valve on your hot water heater, then if it over heats, there is no way to bleed off all of the pressure in an emergency.

That means it's gonna blow and almost nothing will be saved. That is the condition of the USA economy, it is fixing to blow us all the way back to the Stone Age. And the sad part is it is all due to ignorance and stupidity.

Repealing the minimum wage law would bleed off the pressure and the USA would survive with only a miserable rebirth taking place, instead of ceasing to exist. Cry me a river, and the beat goes on.
SIRMANS LOG: 27 FEBRUARY 2014, 1537 HOURS

THE VENTING OF A FREEDOM LOVING AMERICAN!!!
Well it's done, there is no doubt left, the shallow minded liberals has placed the comfort of the welfare state above national security. The choice is no surprise to me. We will soon be like Western Europe, which lacks the military ability to even transport troops to the battle field.

If these liberals keep power, given enough time the USA will be taken over without a bullet being fired. To me it is simple, once the "New deal" programs seized the social and family provider role for itself from the traditional nuclear family head of household the die was cast.

Now, around eighty years later we are fast running out of enough people with the judgment and common sense to remain a free people. We must repeal the evil 1938 socialist minimum wage law to kick the welfare state out of its all powerful family provider role.

It is our last hope; otherwise we will soon be at each others throat to the point that the people will be demanding the iron fist. Like all great nations we are allowing ourselves to be destroyed from within.

The reason you can't survive on the minimum wage is because you have a forced minimum wage in the first place. If you didn't have a forced minimum wage law, out of sight consumer inflation couldn't exist and $5.00 would buy a weeks worth of grocery. Plus, there would be enough jobs for all.

The shallow minded liberals has certainly screwed up this great nation. And if you disagree, guess who held on to the U.S. house of Representative for 40 consecutive years. Also, guess who controls the mass media, education, and almost every institution in America today?

SIRMANS LOG: 24 FEBRUARY 2014, 2105 HOURS

RAISE THE MINIMUM WAGE FOOLS ARE RUSHING IN WHERE WISE MEN REFUSE TO GO.
Anyone that calls for raising the minimum wage doesn't understand a free market place

economy, period. The fact is if the USA is to survive, instead of raising the minimum wage it must be repealed entirely. Vamoose, gone, no more government wage or price control, period.

Large or small any business in America has the freedom to raise wages as high as it see fit. But, the minute the government forces any business to raise or lower wages or prices in any manner we no longer has a free market place economy, period. In my view it is sheer ignorance, you either have a free market place economy or you don't.

Throughout history a true free market place economy has never failed, its boom and bust cycle is a natural process the same as the birth and death cycle. A healthy functioning society is far more than money and how much one makes. In fact, in terms of long term survival trade and bartering is far more important than a currency.

The American Indian and many other societies survived in large numbers and never had a set currency. But, no society has ever survived very long without a strong nuclear and extended family system. Those with money and power hates the boom and bust cycle because they may end up losing everything.

However, nature must have some way of

getting rid of inefficiency, moral decay, and culture rot. Sometimes only the bust cycle can purge out too powerful anti-survival forces like the USA has today.

Just look at the condition of the USA, no law or anything is powerful enough to deal with our problems except nature's boom and bust cycle. The world has been rescued from many dynasties only by nature's birth and death cycle.

I keep yelling and hollering that we must get government out of its seized social and family provider role because that has all but destroyed our nuclear and extended family system. And repealing the evil 1938 socialist minimum wage law will allow our nuclear and extended family system to rebound and allow the people to take care of themselves.

A long over due bust cycle is approaching on the horizon and without a strong nuclear family system we can't survive it. I am blessed with this great wisdom and I see it so clearly, that is why I plead so hard that we must get prepared.

We must repeal the minimum wage law, that will restore our strong nuclear and extended family system, our culture, and at least some bartering capacity to survive. Otherwise, we won't have any chance except back to the Stone Age when this teetering economy

totally collapses, soon.
SIRMANS LOG: 23 FEBRUARY 2014, 1452 HOURS

WE HAVE A MOB RULED WELFARE STATE OUT OF CONTROL!
Extreme political polling is the worse thing that can happen to a free country. It defeats the reason to have a republic. None of the founding fathers wanted a pure democracy because they all knew in reality it is mob rule with the most flamboyant and smoothest talkers chosen as leaders.

That is the reason they all insisted on a republic form of government. However, that was long before extreme political polling came along. These were men of great depth and wisdom they knew that the general public is almost never right on anything.

As a rule the general public is uninformed, emotional, and lacks patience, which is a terrible way to govern a nation. So, they all thought by establishing a republic form of government the fear of a mob ruled nation was put to rest forever. Now, lets fast forward to the year of our Lord two thousand fourteenth year, we are almost totally mob ruled all because of extreme political polling.

In a republic the people are suppose to choose leaders that will lead and educate the general public on what is in the best interest of the nation and its long term survival. But today it is just the opposite; we have politicians using extreme political polling to pander to the whims and special interest of the general public.

Even worse, we no longer have a free press standing guard, they are cheer leaders at the socialist parade. A statesman is someone that can only be found in the history books. The thing that the founding fathers feared the most has come to pass, our leadership is chosen from the most flamboyant, smoothest talkers, and those with the best gift of gab and ability to pander to the voters.

Sorry Benjamin Franklin, Sir, we have lost the great Republic you and the founding fathers left for us to keep and safe guard. What we have now is a mob ruled welfare state out of control. To be enlighten read Freddie L Sirmans Sr. books, it is all there.
SIRMANS LOG: 16 FEBRUARY 2014, 2045 HOURS

THANK GOD! FINALLY! A PLAN TO BOOM THE USA ECONOMY AND CREATE JOBS, JOBS GALORE!
Listen up America; we are on the brink of losing our great USA. So, I felt the need to write this article on what I feel must be done to help save this great nation. Folks, I am a

writer and not even a famous or well known one at that. I have no power or influence to speak of.

I am just a lone handicapped neurotic self-made two finger pecking writer. Some even feel I'm off my rocker, too extreme, and should be totally ignored. Maybe so, but the proof of the pudding is in the taste, be your own taster.

Anyone familiar with my writing knows that I have long advocated the repeal of the evil 1938 socialist minimum wage law. And I also think government should abandon its role as a mass social and family provider. I am sure those are the two main things that have brought the USA economy to the brink of total destruction. And by the same token those two things have bred the USA into a government dependent nation.

I know it's futile to expect my ideas to be taken seriously; still I feel I have done my part just by sharing. I believe the mass infusion of government money on an "Individual basis" is what's destroying the USA economy. Doing that destroys the natural balance between the merchant (seller) and the consumer (buyer), thereby causing cost of living inflation.

The reason the middle class is not spending is they don't have the money because of cost of living killing inflation. With that being the case to me the solution is obvious, get the "Individual basis" out of the formula.

There are many ways to do that, in the past I have suggested government set up its own government run commissaries, housing, and clinics. And require the use of tokens or script for all who qualifies. However, I no longer advocate using that system because of start up and other costs.

What I now recommend is government setup a contract type system to separate government "Individual Basis" spending from the national free market place economy. This new recommended system is ready to go and can be put in into place immediately, everything is practically already in place. The use of food stamps is well established.

Remember the key to eliminating the "Individual basis" from the national free market place economy is separation. So, all government has to do is contract with retailers for set aside stores for food stamp use only.

That will stop the upward cost of living spiral in its tracts, then the buying power of ones paycheck will buy much, much more and the middle class will be able to save again.

Also, these government stores must accept

only EBT or some other type of government card or it will defeat the purpose. Once the government stores are up and operating then EBT and other government cards can only be used in those stores.

This separate retail system could be tested in one state, e.g. Michigan. And if successful, then extend to housing and clinics, and if still successful then go nation wide. Without a doubt this system will boom the USA economy and put people back to work on a large scale, plus save our dying economy.

However, don't hold your breath, politics is in everything, and what I believe will save the economy and this great country may never see the light of day.

However, the cold hard fact is either the USA takes this plan serious and change course, or I will guarantee you the USA will soon be sold off piece meal to foreigners. Being $17,000,000,000,000,000,000 in debt makes the USA a beggar, and you know the old saying: Beggars can't be choosey. There is no doubt about it the country will soon be sold off.
SIRMANS LOG: 25 JANUARY 2014, 1702 HOURS

USA SURVIVAL ANALYSIS JANUARY 2014

Evil 1938 Socialist Minimum Wage Law Is Destroying USA

Here is my Freddie L Sirmans, Sr. analysis on the state of the USA survival. I will say up front the USA can be saved as a free nation with private property rights and individual freedom still intact. But, I don't believe the USA has a snowball chance in hell of surviving another five years as a free sovereign nation with the course we are currently on.

I believe because of our debt ($17,000,000,000,000,000,000) and reckless spending the USA will be sold off piece meal to foreign nations. Our government at all cost will try to hold on to its social and family provider role. If not that we will lose our individual freedom and private property right and come under some type of authoritarian rule.

This liberal induced welfare state has run it course, it's over, something gotta give. Reality have set in and will not be denied. Let me say again the USA can be saved. We have two major political parties, However, I am an independent with conservative leaning. The USA is the only home I know and my whole focus is the survival of my beloved country.

I have voted Democrat many times, I even voted for Jimmy Carter and George McGovern. In my analysis I will stay with the terms liberals or conservatives. So brace yourself and hang on. I feel the liberal mindset has all but destroyed this great land of the free and home of the braved that the founding fathers laid out.

Of course the liberals will totally disagree with me on this, they believe they have greatly helped the poor and made life easier for everyone. And, I will not for one second disagree, who could disagree with that, because it is true. But, that is the trap and where my great depth and wisdom comes into play.

I have said it before and will say it again. The only way government can help the very poor and needy without destroying our culture, our economy, and eventually our country is to establishing government run commissaries, houses, and clinics with the use of coupons or scripts for all who qualify.

Government spending on an individual basis must always be kept separated from the national economy or inflation will eventually spiral out of control. It is on the individual basis that government money destroys the natural balance between the merchant (seller) and the customer (buyer).

That is what ignites and causes inflation in a free market place. And is the reason the cost of living (prices) far out distances the earnings from the workers labor.

Evil 1938 Socialist Minimum Wage Law Is Destroying USA

Government can spend all it wants and it won't drive up the cost of living as long as it is not handed out on an individual basis. That is why the use of coupons or script is a must to keep government individual spending separated from the real economy. And things like food stamps or whatever is used must never be spent with the free market place merchants. because that is what is driving the cost of everything for the working man/woman out of reach now.

Back to the truth about liberals helping the poor. Sure they help the poor, but, my God, at what a price. Their method is leaving almost no survival tools in place after four generations. We have almost no strong nuclear and extended family system left. We have almost no sense of morality left.

Plus, we have almost no small farmers and home gardeners left to provide emergency bartering capacity if money become worthless, which is highly likely. Morality today means same sex marriages and killing in the womb on demand, if that don't mean suicide to long term survival I'll be a monkeys uncle.

It is like selling your sole for riches and pleasure. Destroying the system itself should always be avoided, but that is exactly what the liberal's mindset has done. They took the course of least resistance and have destroyed a system that has served mankind for over 6000 year.

All of our eggs are in one basket, this phony economy could collapse any day now and there are no survival tools to keep the USA from regressing all the way back to the Stone Age. The two deadly and unforgivable sins the liberals committed are number one they seized the social and family provider role for the government itself.

That act took away the survival need for the strong nuclear and extended family system. According to nature's supreme law of natural selection everything that exists must have a survival need or it starts ceasing to exist. The second deadly sin was to enact and put in place a evil 1938 socialist minimum wage law.

That act gave the government total power and control over private property rights, all production, and the distribution of products. In fact the welfare state couldn't exist without the minimum wage law. It would have no way of corrupting the free market place by inflating the money supply enough to continue reckless spending.

Ninety nine percent of the general public sees the minimum wage law only in terms of the size of their pay check, but that is a facade that disguises the absolute power it gives the

Evil 1938 Socialist Minimum Wage Law Is Destroying USA

government over free enterprise. So, as for who can save this great country, in terms of liberals saving it, ridicules, first the country must be saved from the liberals.

Now, as to the role of the conservatives, bless their hearts they means well. But, they don't even come close to being willing by hook or crook to match liberals for getting power. Plus, conservative think they can cut spending and still save our welfare state, trust me that ain't gonna happen.

It's far too much water over the bridge in my view for this welfare state to ever be saved. Besides, politically speaking all spending cuts is going to do is guarantee liberals stay in power. My suggestion for conservatives is go with the flow until you get in power and then repeal the minimum wage law.

But, do like the liberals never tell your true intentions just get in there and repeal it. The problem with my suggestion is: The conservatives totally disagrees with me, they have been seduced and think they need to save this welfare state and if anything raise the minimum wage, not repeal it. Government must be returned to its role before the "New deal," repealing the minimum wage law will do that.

So, like I have said before only a miracle can

save the USA from total doom. However, I do believe in miracles.

THE END

**Freddie L Sirmans, Sr.
Website: FLSirmans.com**

www.ingramcontent.com/pod-product-compliance
Lightning Source LLC
Chambersburg PA
CBHW071235170526
45165CB00003B/1102